I0840990

TRUMP VS. GROUP

by Karen Kellock Ph.D.

Manual for Superior Men

A complete theory based on Einstein physics,
Political Psychology, Systems Theory
and Archetypal Psychiatry.

FORMULA

All success attraction
All disease obstruction
All recovery elimination

You must fast on all three

OBSTRUCTIONS:

People
Habit
Food

TRUMP VS. GROUP

The superior man bows to no one but the weak bow down to their every need no matter how ridiculous: that's the people pleasing sickness. It keeps us mentally unstable: entrenched from early development it's hard to get rid of it.   How about your mental health, your safety, your boundaries? They're gone if you people please: something in the future you'll look back on and will not believe.

TRUMP VS. GROUP
Preface

TRUMP VS. GROUP

Is This Not You Too?

PEOPLE PLEASING SICKNESS
CALLOUS DISREGARD
CAN YOU TRULY TRUST THEM?
BOUNDARIES AREN'T TAUGHT
THE POWER OF NO
PEOPLE COME AND GO
COMMIES MAKE IT ABOUT OTHERS
WOMEN NEED PROTECTION FROM FRIENDS
HYPERSEXUALITY
THEORETICIANS SEE THRU THE MESS
MOTHER CONVICT-MAKERS
BE WISE: FEAR GOD'S CURSE
SUDDEN BLACKENING OF RESPECT
DYADS, TRIADS, JEALOUSY TRIANGLES
DO I WRITE TO NOT GO MAD?
FAMILY CAN BE WORST ENEMY
EVEN DICTATORS HATE TRAITORS
VELVET GLOVE OR IRON FIST
HILLARY WANTS TO KILL BABIES BEFORE DELIVERY
LIBERALISM THE DEFAULT SETTING
AMERICANS ARE FED UP WITH STUPIDITY
DEMS ARE HYPOCRITES OF THE WORST KIND
GREATNESS AND HOPE OR PETTY DOPES?
MODERN WOMEN LACK TENDERNESS
ABHORRENT HILLARY—TO THE PILLORY!
KLEPTOCRATS DISMANTED AMERICA
PATRIOTS FEEL DEEPLY UNLIKE THE CREEPY

TRUMP VS. GROUP

Is This Not You Too?

HATE CRIME DEMEANING DIGNITY?
DAILY OUR SENSES ARE OFFENDED
WE'LL NEVER FORGET YOU LOVED HILLARY
AMERICANA WAS WONDER OF THE WORLD
THE LEFT LOVES SEXUAL IMPROPRIETY
CREEPY KIDS ATTACK "MIDDLE CLASS MORALITY"
TO LIBS, ENTITLEMENT JUSTIFES FRAUD
ANTIFA ALWAYS ATTACKS FIRST
FAMILIES DIVIDED OVER TRUMP
ELIMINATE TRUMP HATERS NOW
IT'S EASY TO BE MISANTHROPIC
CROOKS HAVE BEEN IN CONTROL
SOLITUDE IS BETTER, BELIEVE ME!
SON OF A PORNOGRAPHER AND PROSTITUTE
MULTITUDE OF JEALOUS ACCUSERS
OLD AMERICA: STATES YOU FLY-OVER
LIBERALISM MADE US INSANE
HIX POLITIX OF DEMS AND CLINTON
OBAMA THE MUSLIM DICTATOR
LIBERALS ARGUED WITH EVERYTHING WE SAID
IT'S TYRANNY OR RENAISSANCE
HOLLYWOOD SCUM DIVIDE THE COUNTRY
LEFT HATES OUR TRADITIONS AND CUSTOMS
THE DOUBLEMINDED ARE UNREWARDED
CRY BABIES/DUMMIES DON'T KNOW HISTORY
HIX POLITIX UPDATES
HOMESTEAD UPDATES

Preface

TRUMP VS. GROUP

YOUR DISCOVERY: WHAT IS REAL VALUE?

Most are conditioned to believe value is on the surface—the way it looks is the way it is: nonsense.

Value is deep. That's why you've missed great men cuz you're lost in the shining glitter of fake, amen.

They always pegged me immediately. They never looked deeper for real value so I didn't either see.

Re-see YOU. Cuz much of what you think is you is not, you've been world conditioned like a robot.

Value as Applied to Psychology

Don't talk too much cuz your words bely the truth—the low life level reflected in words uncouth.

Soon memory's all in the begone. The things important today vaporize into nothing--zero, none.

Time to let the inherited--imputed--shame go. You've self-forgiven & resumed a new life ya know.

I have suffered a great number of catastrophes and most never happened. Mark Twain

THE PAIN CONTAINS ALL YOU NEED

TRUMP VS. GROUP

Everything you need to learn is contained in the pain but you gotta feel it not relapse to subdue it.

The one question should be: what do I need to learn so I don't go thru this again? That's it see.

Don't be like Mary who goes thru the pain cyclically over and again but never learns the lessons.

Embrace the pain of withdrawal: get into it. Live it like you never feel it again cuz you won't.

She dresses to show her "feminine energy" but it's only broken consciousness she displays.

Maybe a little boy wants all that skin but a king will not, you'd just be embarrassing him.

This is you taking partial responsibility for a soul tie. You brought it on greatly by your naivete.

Your appearance shows you've been indoctrinated by toxic male society [to be unlearned quickly].

You gotta show your body to attract a man: wrong. You gotta live like a wife wanting to get along.

A king doesn't want a groupie conformist. He wants an individual like God created, not a feminist.

WORLD VALUES ARE WRONG

Women must realize they're taught wrong and are doing wrong. It's hard with so much confirmation.

Because you were taught wrong and did wrong you got results which were beneath you hon'

You reject the world's false metrics about the value of things, including YOU in their perceiving.

TRUMP VS. GROUP

The world puts a value on you for youth, size and sexuality but you've rejected this instantly.

World values are carnal & temporal: fleeting, passing away, lasting for a tiny span of time that's all.

False metrics: If you're not a certain age, size or sex appeal forget you girl-- it's all very cruel.

FALSE METRICS ARE A HEX

What is life like after a size 6? After middle age has passed? It's really ridiculous: rise above it.

Life is about helping each other thru old age not sex--get over this cultural neurosis/current rage.

False metrics make you lunatics. They won't go to your instagram unless you show a little skin/sex.

You must reject all that. Your value isn't in your youth in fact traditionally it's the elder seen as best.

Your value from your size? Are you kidding, think about how utterly ridiculous yet that's it, aye.

Your value in youth, when wisdom comes with age? Only a sick society won't value the sage.

The manchild says why date a 40 year old when you can have a 16 year old? False metrics are cold.

YOU BROUGHT SEX RIGHT INTO IT

"I have a brain, I have a good heart" but you brought sex right into it first off sweetheart you tart.

Your value is never in sexuality. It's no longer about proliferating the race but pure carnality.

TRUMP VS. GROUP

There's great value to sex if you're married but not something you lead with in a single world.

Stirring a man up sexually won't enable him to see intellect or creativity, it's all about sex see.

The soul tie was initiated by you insofar as it palliated a trauma bond or the sex brought him along.

Stop saying you were hypnotized by Svengali, you used sex immediately cuz that's all we knew see.

We swam in muddy waters since age 6 in this sick culture. Sex was nothing: the devil's lure.

No miss, you gotta take responsibility for this. Ladies put on the breaks, man falls in love quick.

JUMPING TO OBEY TOXIC MEN

She jumps to obey he who won't commit but with a good man she has problems to submit.

Find roots to the stronghold making you compliant to abusive commands of toxic men.

Now unlearn this programming and see things right. That noncommittal man is a blight.

Girls: You will never please toxic male culture cuz the oppressor will never empower.

You're too fat, too skinny, too dumpy or too dowdy: there is always something you see.

Oppressors never empower oppressed. Do everything you can they still have you hoppin sis.

NEW SEASON OF SELF-DISCOVERY

TRUMP VS. GROUP

Meet Self thru self-discovery, self-definition and self-development--no one else involved.

A new season when you have no one in your life but you. This self-discovery is wonderful too.

A new season finding out what you like and don't like--that creates a real health in you finally, aye.

What you move away from, what you can't stand, what it all means, how much you wanna be alone.

Until you see thru healthy eyes you will always ascribe value to trash, lacking discernment of assets.

LET YOUR HISTORY DEFINE YOU

Meet yourself by going thru your history. What you've gone thru makes you who you are honey.

Why you accept the things you do, why you don't: your therapy can be done this way you know.

Being invaded by a gang of boys made me who I am, it's embedded so much I think it's God's plan.

A striving for identity after treachery made me this way, working all night fulfilling God's plan ok.

Being a desert rat in the wilderness for 30 years made me this way: a loner who loves to isolate.

Being a nonconformist to female culture: Cinderella syndrome, two lib sisters colluding with mother.

From this you can see how history molds us and when it's all said and done, was it not God's plan?

SEASON OF SELFISHNESS

TRUMP VS. GROUP

You gotta have a Season of Selfishness where it's all about you. You deserve it after this hullabaloo.

The season of self-discovery/development will set you up for a wonderful life after overcoming strife.

You can't really appreciate another until you know who you are--at your core. It's exciting for sure.

Questions for self: what lingering hurts do I allow to define me? Intrusive thoughts reflect these.

What are your weaknesses, your shames and guilts? These are roadmaps, revealing psych-quilts.

I wanted to be alone but society judged me harshly for that, now I find it's my greatest asset.

YOUR PEARL VS. MEN AND WORLD

Poisoning and preventing you from being functional: that's what you're delving into/finding out.

What of your contribution to the world, aye! Now you see sick relationships were a waste of time.

All that energy you put into sick relationships was wasted. Now you have priorities instead.

Discovering your personal priorities is a major blessing. It changes the whole map to start pursuing.

These were not the priorities of your frenemies and that was a painful collision of personalities see.

You kept pressuring me to do what I didn't want to do. Those days are over cuz I'm different from you.

You chose wrong because not knowing who you are you accepted anything that came = despair.

TRUMP VS. GROUP

I felt crazy with confusion until I realized I wanted a formal life style, not drop-ins or hangers around.

Know thyself and life will become wonderful, interesting, productive and EXCLUSIVE.

Immaturity is torture when accepting anything that comes cuz you have no boundaries in sum.

Your best education was your horrible life without boundaries. Now you have em, expect victory.

Must learn to appreciate actual value. How to get yours back: stop playing a losing game Sue.

CUT LOSSES, FEEL PAIN, MOVE ON

When you see you're losing, know when to hold/when to fold and embrace the pain of withdrawal.

The pain does not last, it's temporary. Delay seeking permanent solutions just endure it see.

You must unlearn the old female slave conditioning and relearn/strive for your own godly perfection.

You say you'll abide office hours until noon then you bother me at 9 or ten, a boundary busting man.

How stupid to leave someone for greener pastures--you don't know for sure if it'll turn out better.

Meet yourself formally, using all that energy you put into connecting to people and also manipulating.

The enormous energy going into people will now go into self-discovery and it will fascinate you surely.

FASCINATION OF SELF-DISCOVERY

TRUMP VS. GROUP

Find what you do best and marry your purpose. What you've been put here for, now just do that.

Learn to appreciate actual value. What attracts you: The glitter, the flash, what's on the surface?

Appreciation of flash is the difference between you and the jeweler who appreciates actual value.

He drives up in a ferrari but can't afford it--you're impressed cuz it's all the imagery around it.

Actual value may be quiet, restrained, simplistic but you want the ornate, loud, society-worshipped.

Start to look deeper. Don't accept surface flash anymore or anything society values for sure.

Learn to appreciate actual value and stop being excited about profile--in other words, get some style.

DEVELOP PERSONAL STYLE

Develop personal style or be embarrassed later from swimming in muddy waters and looking stale.

Write down somewhere: you're enough as you are, no need to perform, be pressured only from inner.

You should only compete with your inner view of the best version of your self, increasing for life.

Pause, and re-think "ME". What do I want, what makes me happy--not how culture has conditioned thee.

Lastly, intend to not be angry. Cuz you've gone thru all this/been broken you give an angry impression.

As God brings you into NEW CIRCLES you don't wanna have that anger hangover from old battles.

TRUMP VS. GROUP

You're now meeting people who treat you differently. For what another man did, don't make em pay.

Now let that something shift in your life as God does a new thing in you with great prosperity too.

LORD WILL HAVE TO STOP IT

Lord I promise I'll retire if You stop the flow. I'm tired as a constant spigot but its up to You ya know.

Two more pages and the Creative Act is complete: fifty years and 70,000 proverbs to make ya think.

Just two more pages and a tidal wave is going thru my veins: I'm finally done/that minute has come.

I'm finally done, my time has come. One never knows until that minute but I sense it even the mon.

TRUMP VS. GROUP

PEOPLE PLEASING SICKNESS

Overwhelmed we felt powerless or took on learned helplessness and became people pleasers.

We bow down to their every need no matter how ridiculous: that's the people pleasing sickness.

The people pleasing thing is entrenched from early development and it's hard to get rid of it.

People-pleasing: offering compassion, looking the other way. At one point these aren't ok.

How about your mental health, your safety, your boundaries? Gone if you people please.

What's at stake? My own value/peace of mind as a human being. I don't need to please the fakes.

Were you told to people please, to thus disregard your own valid emotions and sensitivities?

I actually let em get me up at midnight to fix them and their buddies a meal-- nothing I wouldn't do.

CALLOUS DISREGARD

We're either stuck in the old mindset or transforming, that's how to see the sly sister thing.

Having cleared out old matrices we now have a brand new perspective of wisdom/knowledge see.

TRUMP VS. GROUP

I thought I'll do it for them then go back to sleep. Instead they hated my lack of self-respect.

People pleasing is something you look back on and can't believe. It busted your morals and boundaries.

The more you people pleased going against your will the more wisdom you have now you're healed.

Whatever your boundaries & sensitivities you were to lay it down and let em trample over your crown.

You're to lay down your life so they can do whatever they want even take over your house.

Such supreme entitlement of evil children in their fifties who don't respect property/boundaries.

No empathy, no consideration for your wants: the communist spirit and other new age thoughts.

Callous disregard for anything you think, feel or want. You only exist for their benefit, chumps.

People pleasing keeps you mentally unstable. It's like giving yourself away then letting in evil.

CAN YOU TRULY TRUST THEM?

At the end of the day, could I trust my sisters? No, they were my worst enemies and persecutors.

These malevolent tendencies must be faced and discussed. No more family togetherness guff.

Jesus brought a sword to DIVIDE families and in our own house are our worst enemies. Treachery

Around will signing time you really see it, esp as they garner professional support from shysters.

TRUMP VS. GROUP

Did I trust my aunts or other relatives? I noticed they weren't reciprocal, low quality, imbalanced.

I trusted that whatever evident good was coming to me my sister would surely block it see.

That was the kind of trust I had. Trust in an unworthy treacherous world where secrets prevailed.

Aging babies: Even though people are old now they see the world as when they were a child.

The same childish, petty competitive strivings of children remain with "mature" adults friends.

Deceptive, secretive, psychologically abusive relationships with people who are dead.

Not words but actions: abuse, betrayal, deception, retaliation, gaslighting, scapegoating.

Then you see: wow, they don't respect me. So I will respect myself and find those who can.

BOUNDARIES AREN'T TAUGHT

My mother never taught me boundaries nor did she have them except she didn't like interruptions.

Brainwashed as a child to feel powerless and unworthy you had no boundaries [very scary].

When you set boundaries on every aspect of your life it is so relieving after being so imposed on see.

You're unworthy--this is embedded in us and it leaves trauma. I see in their faces, child or momma.

This notion is cellular memory which is throughout our whole body. Think of it: you are unworthy.

TRUMP VS. GROUP

Growing up is seeing that people don't respect us as we thought, and don't really love us--hah!

We grow through identification with, we self-actualize through separation FROM. Maslow

Youth do mistreat us and treat us like door mats and walk all over us and impose themselves.

It doesn't feel good, not at all. At this point we do set clear boundaries or we continue to fall.

Boundaries are about you more than other people. What are your standards/limitations?

Where do you put a line in the sand? We MUST have that line somewhere, think about it man.

This is right, this is wrong. This is acceptable, this is unacceptable. Know thy selves people.

Your boundaries are for YOU: your protection, safety, mental health and emotional well being.

Setting boundaries opens you up to whole new worlds of adventure and learning. Try it and see.

THE POWER OF NO

People take us off goal or distort the radar. They distract from destiny and cause trouble for sure.

This is why the most important word in the vocabulary is "NO!". Stay on the beam never to roam.

Saying NO to the outer world opens you up to the INNER world which is an elite adventure.

Keep this central: If anyone disrespects your boundaries you show them the door now.

TRUMP VS. GROUP

You do have value though they said you had none. You call back your power after being held down.

Your divine purpose is to leave your dark cocoon and fly away to greatness. Yes, you must leave it.

You're not meant to be stuck in broken dead toxic relationships, you're meant to soar over it.

You are meant to expand yourself and that means breaking free from unhealthy relationships.

We don't wanna be bitter over our past hurt and trauma but to expand from/use it for betterment.

Where there is a grateful heart, miracles unfold. That's me today after reconciling patterns of old.

One day you realize it had to happen in that way to give you the lessons to grow far better ok.

PEOPLE COME AND GO

People come and go so what have you gotten out of it? Do things that are eternal, deep, spiritual.

We want to OWN our life. We want to step into our own power, speaking confidently thru clear minds.

You can't do that if your energy's centered here, there, everywhere. Bring it in to a rod of power.

Don't fear loneliness, go towards the void. Make an empty space so God can fill it in/anoint it.

To know our emotions are genuine, authentic and valid despite how they've been invalidated.

You can't control them but you can control who you're with now and that's all you gotta know.

TRUMP VS. GROUP

We now surround ourselves with those who care for and respect us, who love and give us dignity.

I tried being a peacemaker but that was impossible in an imbalanced psychopathic relationship.

Respect & trust. At the end of the day, could I trust my own mother? No, she was my worst gossiper.

COMMIES MAKE IT ABOUT OTHERS

Commies: They make it not about you but about other people. "For the greater good" is EVIL.

It's your fault if you get lackadaisical about your boundaries since they're the main thing.

If they get in to hurt you it's your fault you had no boundaries, tho' that's a reaction to trauma.

Trauma brings PTSD and intrusive memories. People are cruel and the effects last a lifetime see.

No lady can live in disorder. Shut your eyes/put up with it? Only if two houses but even then, reject it.

When single it was like a bull's eye was painted on me. It's a jungle no different from the wild see.

When single I had to struggle for the right to privacy. In a battle to be free it was like they owned me.

If single you're a sitting duck. Men too need to block influences that degrade em/get em stuck.

WOMEN NEED PROTECTION FROM FRIENDS

All she wants is a real man to take care of things. But if in sin he slides into ruin and treachery.

Taking care of the manly stuff around, all those things in the tool room I don't know about? HEAVEN.

TRUMP VS. GROUP

Life of the mind: 20 years ago i didn't know a thing then everything sped up at the rate I'm taking it in.

A real woman appreciates a real man/all the differentials that make the opposite sex fascinating.

It's fashionable for women to hate men. They initiate divorce 80% of the time, a dangerous trend.

Hypersexuality comes from trauma also. Boy does that explain those I knew they called assholes.

As the elder body RECEDES the temporal lobes EXPAND to reveal ETERNITY: a phantasmagoria man.

A man just seems to be born with the knowledge of everything at Home Depot--I admire them ya' know.

The ability to love/submit to a man comes with age altho' it used to be it was taught before engaged.

The ability to love a man and not fight with him--boy is this a lost art. I'm afraid it's gone forever.

Emasculated and humiliated by their liberal wives: it's happening across the land--men despised.

HYPERSEXUALITY

Hypersexuality is ONE natural outcome from TRAUMA and thusly a world of understanding opens up.

With TRAUMA nature compensates with hypersexuality to perpetuate the race--makes total sense to me.

Oprah Winfrey said as a teen she was totally promiscuous and didn't even know it. Trauma I'll betcha.

You can be a blind compulsive eater or promiscuous bottom-feeder all from trauma way earlier.

TRUMP VS. GROUP

After the trauma the traumatizing schools chime in with "sex" instruction which is really pure porn.

I can hear people yelling at me. Women--like I'm in a cage or something with no way of escaping.

One can feel desperately in love and it's still trauma-based. It just has to be tested out I guess.

Tho' her hyper-sexualized response was purely drug and trauma-based she's still seen as a disgrace.

She's done. She had her brief time in the sun but that's just a respite from what's about to come.

Women think: solve the world's problems by being nice and tolerant but they can't, it's the opposite.

One can be traumatized just by having a liberal mother who's angry or hyper-social, a useless bother.

She's hyper-social to compete or as expected, drawing her away from the home which is best.

THEORETICIANS SEE THRU THE MESS

Freud took cocaine, Jung smoked the herb. Do theoreticians need it or is it a curse?

It's the most callous, heedless, cruel, illiterate, disordered, sexualized, paganized and weak generation.

Once I saw their evil was limitless/a bottomless pit I became terrified of their very presence.

And to think their mothers justify/don't see their own kid's moral insanity is the question of the century.

The mothers create pre-convicts by justifying their every act. I've ran into these liberal moms in fact.

TRUMP VS. GROUP

These crazy social liberal mothers justify the most extreme and absurd bad behavior, ohm!

They "love" people to death. These liberal women don't know what they're talking about sis.

MOTHER CONVICT-MAKERS

They give no moral guidance to teens, they curb no bad behavior, they have complete permission sir.

Many of the "loving" convict-creators are Christian women forgiving without repentance.

Even as I showed mom the broken glass she denied her son did it in total loyalty to a menace twit.

These all-loving liberal mothers have created monsters who reflect them perfectly and it's misery.

These convict-making mothers are often seen in multiple selfie pics because that's what it's all about.

You must avoid all cliques and hate em with a passion. They are liberal, conservatives are alone.

He learned obedience from the things that He suffered. Think about that now--it'll all be worth it.

I shudder when I think of sins of youth. God's a gracious One, He'd have to be that's the truth.

BE WISE: FEAR GOD'S CURSE

Nothing worse than the curse of God. Everything you touch fails/nothing's right/you're seen as odd.

Under the curse of God there's no where to hide as your soul is brought down before the whole tribe.

TRUMP VS. GROUP

Anyone with a magic illustrious destiny like you would naturally have enemies--THE adversary.

You had violent enemies to your soul and that's why it's so grievous looking back but it's all over now.

It's all over--your war. V Day is here--your victory is ensured cuz God has brought you this far.

I am waiting for the divinely promised LINK to produce this great and wondrous work--is it you, sir?

I'm interested in the Holocaust. I relate to that cuz I experienced the blackening of human respect.

SUDDEN BLACKENING OF RESPECT

I experienced the blackening in my own family, divorce due to treachery and the terror of discovery.

I experienced how gossip--from my own sister--could inflame a whole town against me: disaster.

I experienced how suddenly groups can change--instantly--against ONE, the victim of insanity.

Overnight their neighbors turned against the Jews. Instantly though rich they were abused.

Any victim of scapegoatism never trusts humans again because most are enemies, few are friends.

The way you talk to me reminds me of how THEY talked to me and so I say: go away, leave me be.

It is the bleakest feeling having trusted humans and then they turn on you--a gut-wrenching lesson man.

I ended up in the desert all alone without a friend and so HAD to turn to God, my Father in heaven.

TRUMP VS. GROUP

The way you talked to me reminds me of how they talked to me and that'll never happen again see.

I know how devilish and despicable people can be and so when I see/hear it in you it's bye-bye baby.

Take your garish, narcissistic, empty gig and shine your dim blinking light on someone else, I'm out.

The more memories of disrespect build up the more bad events happen cuz of our quickened reactions.

A tiny group of. conservatives in a town full of liberals--it was terrorism and nothing they wouldn't do.

DYADS, TRIADS, JEALOUSY TRIANGLES

Dyads, triads, interlocking jealousy triangles, reputation destruction, serial bullies in the sick family.

One of these days I'll be gone for good and you'll not be able to reach me. No hoovering, it's over see.

Why must you have thousands of selfies? Is it from lack of real content or is it all narcissism of a flea?

PTSD: You were unprotected then, you're fully protected now. People are evil and the dam was down.

You threw me to the wolves and incited them against me as well. It's mighty hard to forget that, do tell.

You think you're so clever and smart but I find it underwhelming and packed with leaven.

I guess you just have a way with human beings and I don't so you win, is that it? No, cuz God anointed.

Don't wanna be a preacher, women are not to preach. I'm happy as a humble poet, that's how I teach.

TRUMP VS. GROUP

Study Holocaust: How the Jews struggled for identity in a world of dehumanization and murder.

Please help dogs/cats/homeless brats. Open your heart cuz you know how they treat the marked.

A beta male feels one way then a whole other way after talking to his liberal wife. It is disgusting.

In liberal systems it's all about cliques: I refuse to partake so will remove myself totally, good luck.

I can't stand your cliques, go to hell. I saw em in churches as the chosen deacon is the most social.

Hitler linked with Muslims/hated Jews. Merkel his daughter lets em in as holocaust continues.

A Muslimized Germany is antisemitic and thus the holocaust continues, it's very clear isn't it.

Study the holocaust, endlessly sickening. It is hard for the consciousness to accept it, a blessing.

DO I WRITE TO NOT GO MAD?

Did I write it so as NOT to go mad or to go mad in order to understand the nature of madness? Survivor

It was the immense, terrifying madness that had erupted in history and in the conscience of mankind.

To be suddenly surrounded by strangers is a persecutory mess experienced by any saint or genius.

Suddenly I didn't know my own family and they didn't know me. A stranger in a strange land see.

It's a torturous punishment: bringing people in on us. A sad and sour intrusion, demographic change.

TRUMP VS. GROUP

Resolve past by seeing it as necessary to bring out your multi-adaptive genius and overcoming muscle.

The more pain you went thru--the more they imposed on you--the more your upshoot to stardom soon.

If you have a talent or knack you'll have enemies lest they can use it to their benefit, that's a fact.

I now see my attraction was based on masochism raising it's ugly head again so delete messages sent.

Just forget it cuz I wager you're too irascible to take a heart chance on and the world's full of em.

I know I fell down but the kinda pain you put me thru really shows what's in you and I kinda am through.

FAMILY CAN BE WORST ENEMY

In like ways, a family can split into two warring camps of one's worst enemies or just one chosen, see.

After studying the holocaust, politics becomes important lest inferior leaders to the same to you quick.

And when you were up but are now down it's the Fallen Hero Syndrome when they KILL you friend.

I say Thank You God for giving me the talent to say all this and even the horrible experiences to learn it.

They start with your spirit. Acting like they own you, or that they even know you--you don't exist at all.

If they're a narcissist they're taking on social values from the world--about you--and you're screwed.

Besides Jesus, Trump is the one giving us hope. Listen to him--a return to reason after that dope.

TRUMP VS. GROUP

Marriage is liberation for a woman so she can create, protected from the rabble and the vermin.

When everyone's a prepper and we explode into innovation it's due to Trump's giving us freedom.

No one feels safe, our time is limited. The enemy couldn't care less, they are so arrogant and bigoted.

God is taking the power of speech away from Hillary. What beautiful justice, now to the pillory.

The biggest threat is Organized Mass Multiple Voting. Otherwise it's a landslide so I'm praying and hoping.

Shame the anthem-sitters for they're no better it's all about principals/not friends of fair weather.

EVEN DICTATORS HATE TRAITORS

Even the worst dictators hate traitors (those who treacherously self-deal) and love martyrs.

Right before Kennedy was murdered he had signed documents eliminating the Federal Reserve.

It's the principals for which we stand. Not whether you're happy with the people in this great land.

Creeps who can't think join in: sitting during our national anthem despite those who died--that's humans.

Great jobs, great neighborhoods, honesty restored. Embrace it: the party of Abe Lincoln and more.

Safety again. Like our childhoods in America: that's after Obama and four decades of trauma.

Jobs will return, prosperity will arise and manufacturing will snap back from every country. Donald Trump

TRUMP VS. GROUP

The "sexist racist homophobe islamaphobe hater/bigot" thing has gone too far--they block your star.

VELVET GLOVE OR IRON FIST

Hardening: Taking the velvet glove off the iron fist is a sign of weakening—the irony of hearts bleeding.

When our New Day comes all collaborators, traitors and gophers will be arrested immediately, no worry.

When does your social justice stand as warrior become just an apologist for violence and murder?

Revitalization Movements show all through history. Led by a charismatic leader it's sudden victory.

Revitalization Movements rejuvenate nations as we see mass readjustment to a new beat.

It was like being stuck in a sewer: You didn't know any better and demons blocked just cuz you knew her.

He speaks the truth. Every word drips with common sense, logic, strength and fighting for patriots, the few.

They think if they can come up with a label for something it becomes reality. How ridiculous, really.

Thirst for Blood: The Revolutionary kills the opposition but then his own (counter-revolutionaries) and it goes on.

Prosperity will rise, poverty will recede and wages will then grow rapidly. Donald Trump

White Guilt: But 95% of murders of blacks are by other blacks! But the BLMs refuse to listen to that fact.

He refused to stand. He disrespected all those who died to ensure freedom in our great land.

TRUMP VS. GROUP

Many of you have put down America for years. You bought the LIE/enabled a criminal takeover of tears.

The corrupt media and leaders are falling apart publicly. This will be over soon so persevere gratefully.

HILLARY WANTS TO KILL BABIES BEFORE DELIVERY

Hillary wants to kill babies days before delivery by pulling them apart: it is so grizzly/this woman is shady.

Lose respect for those blindly following this shady lady. You must for your own sake/to be happy.

Hillary wanted to kill babies two days before delivered. Now, how can you possibly not hate her?

Don't pity those who disrespected and left you alone/forlorned and ruined your rep too, just get armed.

Love those who love you--your True Self is so cool but unfortunately banned by the cruel.

Mental illness/lost genius sets in adapting to nuts. Lost soul: gotta learn to hang on or flunk.

Feminist friends want you divorced. Due to liberalism/globalism that's how far our culture's morphed.

If God raised him up He will also protect him. Hallelujah Lord, fill his cup and banish his foes nonstop!

The only people mad at you for speaking the truth are those living the lie.

Ban her, lock her up for public indecency, put her in mental asylum: How does she get away with this man?

Michelle Obama is the most vulgar first lady we've ever had. Mike Pence

How could you vote for Hillary when she wants to kill a near-infant baby--are you crazy or evil maybe?

TRUMP VS. GROUP

In times of war the laws fall silent. Antonin Scalia

LIBERALISM THE DEFAULT SETTING

Liberalism has been the default setting up to now, with this landslide revolution which is mental.

Americans are the most inventive people on the planet. When Satan rushes in we always solve it.

Americans are innovators and thus we came first: Making God central He blocked the curse.

Julian has exposed the dirty secrets of the powerful: Gross brutality and lawlessness called despicable.

As nations lose liberties and go under tyranny we need whistleblowers so don't treat em terribly.

I can't even blame the liberals who messed with my head. They held their line and my spirit went dead.

The military must know an epic false flag is imminent and are readying (secretly diligent), no?

If you steal a landslide it'll mean war. That many people disappointed--OMG, blood and gore.

Why does she look so mean? What kinda image is she trying to portray--a vindictive brawling wife ain't ok!

The harvest is ripe for evangelism to this generation. They're so dumb it's a turkey shoot, amen?

The guest list is modest but the wedding is historic. Marriage changes life completely/makes one heroic.

Disrespect for cops starts at the top. Even fire fighters are shot--need Trump not these despots!

TRUMP VS. GROUP

I can't imagine what would happen if she stole the election: At this point of Trump-hysteria? Destruction.

He doesn't drink, he doesn't smoke. He's gonna fix our system: put it on the right track/remove the yoke.

AMERICANS ARE FED UP WITH STUPIDITY

People in this country are fed up with stupidity, weakness and not beating ISIS. Donald J. Trump

We're winning no matter what you hear from the media: thieves and crooks. As bad as Hillary: kooks.

Without the corrupt media and corny comics Hillary would be nothing whether politics or economics.

The highest is a preacher to preachers/teacher to teachers. One at a time then they go out there.

Deport criminal illegal offenders quickly--that's the National Security Act, ignored completely.

They'll recall you were always for Trump (before he was popular) and you'll rise up as an officer.

Now we find out Obama stole his election. Dear God, all that time, decline, ruination, loss and destruction!

Either she loses and goes to jail or she becomes queen of the New World Order and criminals prevail.

NFL: One tattooed idiot throwing a ball to another tattooed idiot and that's called "civilization", believe it.

The best laid plans of mice and men often go awry. Robert Burns

Childlike minds really believe that Obama and Hillary are their friends and want to help em.

TRUMP VS. GROUP

They want you broke, destitute, failed. They want you unsuccessful and it's planned in great detail.

DEMS ARE HYPOCRITES OF THE WORST KIND

They are hypocrites of the worst kind. Sick degenerate users/moochers and fools: Satan's tools!

Michelle Obama's guests wrote songs about raping women and she dared to say Trump's the vermin?

Just imagine if Trump were hanging out with rappers bragging about date-rape of drugged women!

Here they sexualize our kids with trash then demonize Donald Trump for it-- just wait for our backlash!

I hate to say we hate but after 8 years of trauma how could we not be irate made to accept this fate?

She's just another silly female on the left--she knows nothing so by default ends a liberal: daft.

Remember what I told you: That if Trump got in, it would be the opposite to what it's been: rich/fun.

Hillary gave them fifteen hundred dollars and an Iphone: "Go to Trump's rally and beat people up—come on"

Them stealing the election is a huge victory as well, since it further discredits them. Alex Jones

Fox has become lackluster/boring compared to the true headlines with proper priorities assigned.

FOX is filled with boring details, speedbumps like Williams or feminist like Kelly--YUK! Fox sux!

Here we're sinking and Kelly's talking about women's feelings. Feminists are stupid and frightening!

TRUMP VS. GROUP

GREATNESS AND HOPE OR PETTY DOPES?

On the one side is greatness and hope, on the other is silliness, false narratives and pettiness by dopes.

Here we're facing the razor's edge--of returning from the brink or sudden sink--and feminists just wanna bitch.

It's the women who are for Hillary Clinton. It's identity politics: that's how shallow and superficial their thinkin'

These feminist are third-rate thinkers. They can't see the whole and mess everything up: messers/stinkers.

MODERN WOMEN LACK TENDERNESS

They lack tenderness, our feminine part. They are cold and heartless and many are little tarts.

The most foul, out-of-control date rape lyrics and more. That's in the Whitehouse/it's a cultural war.

Megyn Kelly is a stab in the back. Feminist hypocrisy hurts sensitives as we face nuclear war (fact).

These crazy feminists will take us into war! Putin wants to be friends but has his line then he'll roar.

A man in the wrong can't stand against a man in the right who keeps on coming. Founder of Texas Rangers

Let justice be done though the heaven's fall. (Fiat justitia ruat caelum, Latin legal phrase)

Hillary is a known warmonger: the pentagon warned us. Very unstable--a vote for her is war (it's nuts).

A billion to take him down won't matter if a landslide later, as God raises standard against God-haters.

TRUMP VS. GROUP

They're incompetent and have no common sense while enforcing a sick will which ruins lives/makes us dense.

From liberalism (A sick mean debauched dumbed/wimped culture) you can escape through Trumpism.
What about that sick devil pres. of Canada, Trudeau? He's just as perverted by liberalism from below.

ABHORRENT HILLARY—TO THE PILLORY!

Hillary wants to kill (two days short of) newborns. Think of that--it's her worst crime/she is abhorrent.

As it all comes out we've no more reason to pout cuz vindication is here so let out a shout!

Enantiodromia is occurring: That's when the bottom becomes the top and the top is self-destroying.

An inversions of systems is happening as we speak. That's where we win and the foe's up a creek.

Voting a third party is voting for Hillary--can't anyone think deeply?--but even the Mormons are this silly.

There is no tenderness in her steely-steady face. There is only shame, corruption and utter disgrace.

How wonderful as we've won and after trouble (a ton) our eyes go out to our future's beautiful horizon!

What a time to be living. Hypocrisy is crashing and prosperity's just beginning as that dark cloud is leaving.

In exchange for amnesty for multiple felonies Huma will be forced to testify against her rejecting lover Hillary.

Organized money is just as bad as organized mob. Donald Trump

We had to go through Obama (to see what we don't want) and it was a trauma but now we've found Trump nirvana.

TRUMP VS. GROUP

Don't gain the world to lose your soul, wisdom is better than silver and gold.
Bob Marley

KLEPTOCRATS DISMANTED AMERICA
We watched the kleptocrats dismantle America and now we want her back.
We weren't watchmen/we were lax.

All bull feminism always ends up looking dumb! We're onto you and it's
weakness/inferiority (crumbs).

The church has turned us into patsies so the bullies run right over us. That's
from being "nice": stop this!

We've gone from a melting pot to a chamber pot in one generation. Michael
Savage

Hillary's Female Pedophilia: We've come to the line--will we accept this as we
did all all else that was vile?

Weiner is ready to sing like a bird to send Hillary/Huma down the river: no honor
with thieves when God delivers!

Trump supplies the catalyst for a world (not just a national) revolution: (Joy,
no more revulsion)!

The archetype of the female pedophile is a bottomless pit and it's horrible to
think about/sick as it gets.

Hillary is making it a women's issue about Trump. Just imagine that but if the
college kids believe it we're sunk.

They're training us to accept less, lowered expectations, a new dark age: a
post-industrial world/feeling caged.

It's not only Clinton but the death of our history--rewriting all of it since the
sixties/influence of hippies.

Men should rule the roost not concede to their feminist wives who scare with
vicious gossip/lies.

TRUMP VS. GROUP

PATRIOTS FEEL DEEPLY UNLIKE THE CREEPY

Anyone who feels deeply--who doesn't have a seared conscience--would be horrified, honest.

By controlling speech they dull our mind and crush our spirit but we can still joyfully pray in private.

You fight for your country and come back being called nazi? It's what's happening in land of the free.

Fake news doesn't tell us what's happening but implant propaganda cuz they have an agenda.

It's all conjecture, not actual facts. False equivalencies with an agenda and that's the news even FOX.

They're dead in the head due to drugs, food, sin and false ideas and thus repentance returns to bliss.

It's not news it's political slants.

Talking lies, omitting or slanting facts is an attack on your country.

HATE CRIME DEMEANING DIGNITY?

The new hate crime is "demeaning dignity"--but that's so subjective it's just means more tyranny.

Laissez-faire attitude of free will: It all looks like hell cuz it's not of God since you do what thou wilt.

Since God is not dirty disorder you're made in the image of the devil and you can't deny it either.

There is crap everywhere, total disorder like a bomb hit it: Does this reflect God, is it spiritually legit?

Christians can't lie (e.g. about gender) so what's it all about: compelling a lie as we're thrown asunder.

TRUMP VS. GROUP

The devil conquered our wonderful country in the sixties and the government are grandkids of those hippies.

Since God raised him up He will also protect him: The savior and fixer of our great country, amen.

DAILY OUR SENSES ARE OFFENDED

Daily our senses were offended, our morals invaded, our logic inverted, our hearts broken and dreams faded.

As soon as they say they're for Hillary you gotta act as though it's Nazis and escape the matrix speedily.

Hillary Clinton, the totalitarian operative under left cover, has fooled us for 40 years but now it's over.

She loved you but feminism made her cold: she accepted the unacceptable (did what she was told).

She was so sweet until she went off to college. Then she was mean, dogmatic, calumnious, horrid.

Those under feminists are driven to mental illness and I can attest to that, self-esteem was a mess.

No worry, returning from the brink is biblical, man. God always shows up at the last minute, then bam!

I see the callousness of liberals in myriad examples that killed the spirit of an angel/blocked channels.

He was shattered by divorce until I said "it was her feminist friends" and his self-hate changed of course.

Their art is silly, meaningless, political, socially hypnotic, pat, redundant, mundane, bland and corny.

Feminists ignore Bill Clinton's rapes and are "shocked" by Trump. What blatant/ignorant hypocrisy: chumps.

TRUMP VS. GROUP

Their glowing reviews are pseudo-intellectual and just for attention. It's embarrassing to know them.

In a dumbed generation it matters not how many "likes" cuz smarts are rare/most are high as kites.

Hillary's rallies were smiles, kisses and hugs. Typical female stuff but NO substance/plans, just crud.

Because of who he is inside and the character of the man, this great leader is devastatingly handsome.

WE'LL NEVER FORGET YOU LOVED HILLARY

We'll never forget you loved Hillary--the baby killer right before delivery! You'll face justice for this treachery.

The dreaded white male is so evil he gave most of the world everything he had. Alex Jones

Social conformity is a demand of the left. They hate individuality (True Genius) and thus aren't blessed.

Michelle Obama hosted people who promote date-rape and gang-rape but she says Trump is morally base.

At the heart of this election was a simple question: Would the people govern or suffer more corruption?

You gotta wall up cuz wicked men want in your house. But if you're a weak woman you'll let em in: ouch.

The lyrics of Whitehouse rappers were: cop killing, drug dealing, date raping and violence against women.

Put a weak woman in power and as the wicked take over your lives will change forever and get worse every hour.

Liberals deliberately create messes/destroy precious things--gives them a thrill/their evil heart sings.

TRUMP VS. GROUP

One candidate was corrupt in political correctness, the other just stuck to the truth, stating the obvious.

AMERICANA WAS WONDER OF THE WORLD

Americana that was the wonder of the world is rising like a phoenix right now. Trumps winning: wow!

Social is a mutual admiration society. It's really embarrassing seeing them slobber but mostly a tragedy.

God uses the flawed. He used sinner Kings to accomplish great things: I hear Trump and am awed.

Though scared to death the sun shines inside, soon to relieve us of eight years of treachery by the snide.

The anti-Trumps are mindlessly swept up by well-funded hysteria and that's what's happening in America.

Men being emotional brittle get their hearts broken and you silly women think they're mean/forsaken.

THE LEFT LOVES SEXUAL IMPROPRIETY

The left has fought for sexual impropriety for decades and yet suddenly are so concerned: charades.

Charade: an absurd pretense intended to create a pleasant or respectable appearance.

Leftists who lie about everything are collaborator trash. You're gonna lose cuz you did it all for Clinton cash.

Trump's being attacked by hyenas and jackals and you won't stand for him in these battles?

Phoniest Obama speech I ever heard, sounds so forced--blah blah, cum bay yah: false dogma=lost charisma.

TRUMP VS. GROUP

Can't stand to see his face, can't stand to hear him. He's the devil and his smooth glibness is sin.

Crime after crime, horror after horror: What kind of a government allows it's people to so greatly suffer?

Liberals find equivalence between a mass murderer and a man who likes pretty women/possible flirter.

CREEPY KIDS ATTACK "MIDDLE CLASS MORALITY"

Creepy kids attack "middle class morality"--something they heard like the script "justice and equality".

The leftist's era is fading. All over we're sick of this false ideology, so immoral and degrading.

Hell is a place where there is no reason. Dante

TV heads: brains eaten.

Milo isn't conservative he's a provocateur. That's not a good thing cuz it's decency we want, you hear?

Milo is truly obscene when you listen to him. My goodness don't let children hear talk like vermin.

Milo seems like a global operative meant to sully our view of the right and it's a stink and blight.

Liberals see themselves with a self-righteous halo. But debunk their delusions and it gets personal.

Trump says "it's ok to love your country" but they're teaching us to hate our nation, land of the free.

They've been using sports to control people since ancient times. This is no different, over the line.

To hell with the globalist NFL. Dads: Stop watching it and take your kids camping--break this spell.

TRUMP VS. GROUP

They say we're bad for not wanting to watch steroid heads spit on the flag every time, Trump's so right.

Every break's anti-gun, anti-family, anti-Christian. We're not gonna take this treachery anymore son.

Your bread and circuses now disgusts us.

Conservatives like pragmatic policies that work. Liberals just wanna feel good about it (comes first).

TO LIBS, ENTITLEMENT JUSTIFES FRAUD

With liberals, entitlement justifies fraud. Though wrong, their ideology seems right but it's not of God.

All I can do is the best I know how. At least I do something, not act tough like you--ducks in a row.

It's all about rubbing our noses in it, dominating and squatting on top of us while submitting to their tyranny.

To a demoralized person, the facts mean nothing. He is unable to access true information: dumbing.

They prey on our demoralized perception as the "gospel truth" then destabilize our world/call us fools.

Obama ok'd to kill 40,000 horses. Can't you see what a monster he is threatening animals, our values, even houses?

Liberals see males through a feminist lens which is anti-men. It's unfair, brutal, false weights and offends.

We're in the middle of a culture war and the main media's on the other side and it's Trump they abhor.

What we need again is bold preaching on hell and holiness not new age nonsense creating this mess.

TRUMP VS. GROUP

Money buys privacy. Like not having to rent rooms to strangers for lousy money.

The hippies promoted Ameriphobia since the sixties, now old bag Hillary keeps doing it though sickly.

Black cop shoots a black guy--it's white people's fault. With liberal trendies it's prejudice they exalt.

ANTIFA ALWAYS ATTACKS FIRST

The people who attack first are the bad guys and that's Antifa.

Whatever the herd does you go along with it. You gotta judge things by the bible and not ignore it.

Libs create the perception of an epidemic of police going after blacks to kill em--all bull hon'.

You don't hate Trump from his speeches (for he's great) you're just against him cuz the herd it pleases.

BLM given several hundred million dollars--now they're in power teaming with ISIS and other fowlers.

A sign of superiority is not bending with insults--not even flinching cuz you know it's the devil's bitching.

They were cute kids but I don't like anyone after they've gone off to school. They become cruel, called "cool".

Never forget the debate--the most important one in history as we approached the razors edge and our fate.

Effects of our collective hate is sure to take him down sometime for he's not invincible nor sublime.

Youtube has brigades of social justice warriors censuring and demonetizing until you conform.

TRUMP VS. GROUP

Trump made it ok to be politically incorrect so now masses are going through that wedge: the elect!

Blacks, listen up: He didn't care about you--he gave it all to his Muslim buddies, an American tragedy.

Dangerous territory: "Fact checking" is opinion journalism pretending to be heightened objectivity.

The arrogance of Wash D.C. will soon come face to face with the American voter--watch! Donald Trump

FAMILIES DIVIDED OVER TRUMP

Has it come to this--families divided over Trump vs. all the politically correct crap? Yes, so dump.

Desperate, they do more absurd things each day. Grab your seat/watch the show and joyfully pray.

If you're gonna vote that way and be such a dumbass we have nothing in common and I'll be droppin.

I can be the best I can be cuz I got a man to protect me, what do you have (feminist throw-away for free)?

We've gotta stop trusting people just cuz they're cute! Look past looks cuz Lucifer is beautiful and astute.

We must confront immature kids and not let em get away with this as their deception surely increases.

Trust that it's a landmark world revolution. Trump is about protection, borders and nationalism.

They've had internet control for a week: They don't do things right away so we feel false complacency.

Our dumbness will get us as we go along with ISIS and it's the kids--that is my studied hypothesis.

TRUMP VS. GROUP

It's our time to shine, or after this we'll be in decline. That's how it goes in seasons of man and bloodlines.

Paul Ryan is more upset with Donald Trump's locker room talk than the assault on America by Barack.

We reflect our generation but we gotta rise above it. It's sick as it can be with promiscuity--don't be it.

ELIMINATE TRUMP HATERS NOW

Wow--I eliminated ten Trump-haters just today. Feels like a two ton enema getting rid of the dumb fray.

Republican war on women? That's absurd. The war is from the left leading them to hell/isolation.

The war on women is the left leading to abortion and immoral deceptions causing lost affections.

Save me the trouble and leave (this right-wing pinnacle) on the double cause you are expendable.

All the things democrats believe in are immoral and evil. Here's a list of the goals of these crazy people.

Democrats are evil but they may not know it. That's how singed their conscience is--they even love it.

White privilege, what kinda bull is this. And so you give them all mansions and put me in the dust?

Hillary, Bill and Barack don't care because liberals in general don't care about a thing--no lines, only flings.

It's in for women to be violent with their men: Angelina Jolie and Hillary for example, time and again.

I don't care if I only have five friends left. Say something against Trump no matter what and I'll drop.

TRUMP VS. GROUP

You hate Trump so what was the alternative? Hillary, tyranny, guns taken and flooded with the enemy.

Liberals are always feigning great benevolence then thieving behind the scenes. Evil helpers, fiends.

No matter who they are liberals say the same thing cuz it's a script and it's so annoying it gets us ticked.

IT'S EASY TO BE MISANTHROPIC

If you hate everyone it's cuz liberals are everywhere, mockin'--it's been the default setting since kindergarden.

My Donald prayed before the debate and that's why he was so great and never took the bait.

Liberals are communist. They want everything equal and that means taking from you ("sharing") and it's evil.

As people reflect their generation they become morally insane. "Moral sanity": gone/decency is slain.

When you hear "Trump is losing", always think: not true. All bull. Liberal hype/stink.

A well-informed conservative is every liberal's worst nightmare. Elvin Bartley

I dis-friended fifty people, so go ahead--make my day: If you hate Trump that's all you gotta say.

Liberals are always faking great benevolence. But have you ever been betrayed by one, by chance?

Savior of USA raised up by God. Has foibles (called "odd") but when in full power we'll all be awed.

The Hillary supporters are dumb, dowdy and dangerous. They only know she's a woman (though traitorous).

TRUMP VS. GROUP

In contrast to the medieval religion that chops off hands we still have faith in man's humanity to man.

Hillary doesn't care about murdering babies/dismembering abortions: she's a sleaze/moral moron.

Let those envying your thirst for power take note of your fate. You've done yourself in, with hell you've a date.

CROOKS HAVE BEEN IN CONTROL

Criminal Takeover: Crooks have been in control but soon Donald will be on a roll and save America's soul.

Save your energy. Instead of getting mad at a liberal, see it's a script that they all advance (trivial).

Soon Donald will reverse things. Biblically, God shows up at the last minute to save the day. hurray!

We need R and R after eight years of terrible trauma seeing our great country dismantled by Obama.

He handled it perfectly, overcoming resistance which vaporized as his detractors were scandalized.

If woman don't "give in" they really "stand out" bringing great respect despite what he expects.

It is so nice that the shackles have been taken off me and I can now fight for America the way I want to. Donald Trump

Women's scorn, worse than men. They don't forget, comes up time and again. Warning: Don't let her in.

When women rule they can be the worst (but some are cool). We're talking war: not for fools.

I've been under liberal women and really, it was vermin and I shudder to think of it (end of sermon).

TRUMP VS. GROUP

I understand frustrations of men dealing with feminists--It's always horrible as they destroy the nest.

Feminism is the default setting so it's just as hard being lady as having morals and keeping chastity.

Adapting to feminists is the worst. It's cuz they're borrowing a personality not their nature (the first).

Don't give into creepy kids. I know how they pressure but you must stand strong and ignore their fibs.

SOLITUDE IS BETTER, BELIEVE ME!

I'd rather be alone for the rest of my life than ever argue with a lazy lascivious liberal again. Amen.

Adapting to liberals brings mental illness. Only the strongest can withstand it's effects I guess.

Liberals make big bucks cuz they work for the system though it sux and that's why they're arrogant: in luck.

Kids will attack your insistence on decency (no sleepovers, no locked doors) but you must missy.

The pope has endorsed Donald! This is interesting after the morality issue in this recent squabble.

As a psychologist I see no narcissism in Trump whatsoever. It's ok to be proud of your works so clever.

On Nov. 8 Wash. D.C. faces the righteous justice of the American voter and it's about time. Donald Trump

Conservatives relate to Trump on a deep cellular level--to us every word describes angels vs. devils.

Just like children they don't know the difference between right and wrong. Embarrassing, isn't it: the human throng.

TRUMP VS. GROUP

A very exciting day, as Mr. Trump has taken the gloves off and I love his every word! Exhilarating! Oh my!

Christians couldn't vote for Clinton cuz she's for abortion and taking away our first amendment: no options!

Clinton would even kill newborns--that's the progressive agenda, more and more gore the Christians abhor.

SON OF A PORNOGRAPHER AND PROSTITUTE

I hate to impose this on you but it's the truth about this son of a pornographer and prostitute.

Trump wants freedom. Hillary wants world government, unlimited immigration and rule by corporations.

Pat Robertson said he had a vision of Trump at the right hand of God and I believe it/don't find it odd.

Trump is a wonderful man. And you're a creep if you wanted Hillary, a horrible woman so please leave vermin.

Putin has no choice but to war against the attacks of Obama and Clinton but with Trump we'll rejoice.

It isn't freedom to free violent prisoners, it's tyranny--cuz then more control is needed, believe me.

Feminist sisters did it to my mother too: put her down for her old traditions with no respect (so cruel!)

This happened across the land when the new feminism began: your poor parents were attacked, man!

Mom was against it all (abortion, homosexuality, sexually free) and was bashed into drinking and insanity.

The selective outrage from the left about sexual impropriety is more a projection from them, entirely.

TRUMP VS. GROUP

Trump's a nice family man with a love of female beauty and you equate that with that rapist, really?

See reality: If he lost she'd have won and we're dead. Study what she'd do and take note of all she said.

The leftist media are best at promoting rape hoaxes like on campus, disproven X times--just ask us.

Leftist media is expert in concocting fake rape stories but also the expert in ignoring real ones (never sorry).

Multitudes of females will now accuse Donald cuz that's the left media's way (they are simply awful).

MULTITUDE OF JEALOUS ACCUSERS

There will be multitudes of accusers now, thus dulling the impact of real rape accusations we know.

Understand people that if he loses, we're dead. Tell everyone--go ahead--for we live on the razor's edge.

Lies and deception: I don't wanna live in a divide-and-conquer system but renaissance and creation.

Every time they try this crap it blows up in their face. Out of desperation they've lost first place.

They see both as equally bad. That shows lack of morals cuz there's no comparison/we've all been had.

Angelina Jolie lost her looks which come from truth/God. No translucency, looks pasty: lackluster/odd.

Angi Jolie's face shows bloated planes. It's from spouting false dogma, not being true and underlying shame.

Hillary's America: Keep babies alive to get body parts. Dear Lord how far we've fallen into hell/dark arts.

TRUMP VS. GROUP

Mainstream media's stranglehold on propaganda is just about done. They lied all along but with Trump we won.

They say Hill stinks like Obama: hell's fumes and flies. The devil is revealed in ways which we all despise.

I hate the republican party. Trump is an outlier, a dark horse taking it over and it's all for us: making it hearty.

We broke through the mainstream media's blackout on Bill Clinton's rapes. Now we're yelling--great!

Progressives: we don't take the bait. We know what you're doing but just want you out (can't wait).

We put up with enough of that in California. People coming late or not at all-- no more of this, I warn ya.

OLD AMERICA: STATES YOU FLY-OVER

Here in Utah man walks tall. It's Old America, so unlike the coasts where people come late/not at all.

They're a mutual admiration society where one loser praises another: useless vain youth--why bother?

The left uses skewed polls to make their point. Don't acknowledge any of em, they disappoint.

Election Stress Disorder was killing me, knowing what I know: that if she won we'd go under tyranny.

Women want secure borders, safety, law and order. So why would they want Hillary, the welcomer?

They deliberately use rare words. No one knows the meaning: pseudo-intellectuals are for the birds.

Their penchant for using obscure terms reeks of snobbery. It's sophomoric youth doing this, really.

TRUMP VS. GROUP

The more human rights the less likely you'll be extracted from home (with a black bag over head) at night.

It's so embarrassing you think it's great. Have you no class, wisdom, discernment of truth vs. base?

As soon as they say they're for Hillary Clinton you know who they are so don't fight em, just forget em.

It's the most massive, epic, gangsterlike and murdering by one in recent history and she's only begun.

LIBERALISM MADE US INSANE

It wasn't the person who made us insane, it was liberalism which is so false it's a sanity-drain.

The thing about liberals is they enforce their false ideology with tyranny so get ready to be unhappy...

Resistance to tyrants is obedience to God. Thomas Jefferson

Suddenly all the anti-war activists/pacifists want war with Russia. Isn't that an interesting discussion.

Ego-driven and power mad. So bullyish they challenge the nationalist Putin: it's so dangerous and bad.

Seasoned warriors are against war. The world changes when you've been there/seen all the gore.

The world changes when sucker punched by the foe. You see everything differently—that's how we grow.

Ghandi said it: First they ignore you, then they laugh at you, then they attack you, then you win. Amen!

She goes out of her way to be a demon but when the camera's are on she's totally loving and even.

TRUMP VS. GROUP

Why would anyone want war with Russia when they could have peace? It's the left that can't be appeased.

Rules for Radicals: Accuse your opponent of what you are guilty of. It's as simple as that but it gets rough.

Just a little freedom and fabulous wealth is created. It works every time with lower taxes/deregulated.

HIX POLITIX OF DEMS AND CLINTON

Whatever she says goes. She's busy taking notes of how to get back and massive networks to hurt foes.

They vote for who they think will win. It's human nature so these fake polls sayin' she was ahead were sin.

To Hillary Clinton steadiness marks the true leader: making decisions that will kill the outsiders.

First she laughed. But Hillary's new persona of steel cold gaze and even hatred--what to make of it?

Revelation: As soon as she got in she'd become a male. Just to mess with our heads, make us crazy/fail.

What a bunch of bull sayin' "they're both bad". Just shut up if you're gonna be so dumb you cad.

Why women shouldn't rule nations: Either they're warmongers or they tolerate abominations.

Women taking her side last night, saying "he encroached" are just showing who they are: dumb toast.

They are clearly floundering, ramping up fake assaults on Trump each week to distract from wiki-leaks.

Not strong enough to be themselves, they slip down to the popular groove and become evil elves.

TRUMP VS. GROUP

You tell by what they write they have nothing inside but sometimes they chirp a slogan and it's snide.

They compare America to utopia and say "it doesn't measure up" so create hell holes/blow everything up.

Getting mad at every dummy you meet will take all your precious energy since they're all doublespeak.

Stop spouting off you liberal creeps. For short-term fame your career is over cuz we're the power peeps.

OBAMA THE MUSLIM DICTATOR

A Muslim dictator destroyed USA and we never protested. Now a guy wants to save us and we can't accept it?

The lying deaf and dumb virtue signalers of the left: if we don't stop them it's the end of the west.

Our nation' s best and brightest have been brainwashed into our dumb and dumbest. Pamela Geller

At this time we see massive mental illness: Stockholm syndrome, confirmation bias, lying to us.

In such turbulent times Trump gives us peace of mind. He's not a smiling ineffectual wimp like the other guy.

Wholesome Americana thrives despite the vicious left. So who is God blessing--can you guess?

There's a glorification of wickedness on the left. It's so sickening--no wonder we're worn out and bereft.

Alpha isn't criminal, it stands for what's right and goes against peer pressure: that's true might.

The left hates the west, Christianity, prosperity and open/free societies.

TRUMP VS. GROUP

Hillary stole but still lost. Progressives think nothing of fraud cuz their "higher goal" is worth the cost.

Election gave us gumption to blaspheme the 60's saints (Hillary) and their religion of hollow progression.

Liberals got what they wanted (can you imagine this): we can kill our babies. That's how cold, dark, shady.

Liberals laughed at our morals, our restraint. They tried to bring us down to their level and not be saints.

LIBERALS ARGUED WITH EVERYTHING WE SAID

Liberals argued with everything we said. Their guidebook to bring us down: confuse, destroy, wreck our plans.

They rained on our parade and took the wind out of our sails. It was all so depressing walking on nails.

They always wanted to control. If unawares this was a terrible snare but resistance built muscle/let em stare.

Liberals were so smug and arrogant. They laughed in our face, they called us stupid but they were "excellent".

How can I sweep it under the rug-with-a-hug after you caused me undue pain for 8 years by being so dumb?

It's not just about Trump: The liberals have been in control of our reality for decades: dirty, base, cold.

People lost all refinement and dignity. They became dirty and even felt pride about it: easy, flirty, floozy.

I want to be part of a Renaissance not a controlled paradigm. I want creative freedom, all mine.

Trump wants to incentivize/cut taxes for the black community--oh, isn't he as horrible as he can be?

TRUMP VS. GROUP

The criminality of the democrats is linked to media and the stars. Hollywood has degraded us so far.

Race pimps and crybabies are losing steam--all based on fallacy cuz things are not what they seem.

Hillary's machine (celebs, activists, hacks) so devoted to getting her elected are shocked at the true collective.

IT'S TYRANNY OR RENAISSANCE

It's tyranny (what it's been) or Renaissance (an explosion of prosperity and creativity: innovation).

There is no pay-gap: Women are paid as much as men.

We're now in the driver's seat. So now just party on, ignore the rioters and get ready for the future, a treat.

What America is really all about: leaving people alone. It's about the individual happily on his throne.

They call us all "Russians" cuz we wanna cut taxes and we care about our veterans.

Zero taxes and major development for black areas--and they say Trump's a racist and bad for America?

Moral relativism crushed our ability to feel. We lost empathy and became selfish, debauched/would even steal.

It's so bad we can't copy any part of it. We must become Puritans-the other way--as our country began when fit.

When people lost morals they also lost excellence and many became like trash, indecent and dense.

Now we can return to true class, like when things were nice. When they were excellent, sweet spice.

TRUMP VS. GROUP

The greatest part is not being bullied anymore. We've won/we're right and they're wrong: media whores.

Those 8 years were terrible: Waking up every morning with dread, fearing we'd end in a camp or dead.

Renaissance is about flowering of the free human will. It built America but liberals want to kill it still?

Under Trump more than half won't pay taxes. Such a bad man, isn't he? The anti-Trumpists know nothing/are asses.

HOLLYWOOD SCUM DIVIDE THE COUNTRY

Hollywood scum trying to divide this country say "whites are inherently bad/racist": This is the bigotry.

It's not just about Trump but the last 40 years of being on the begging end with liberal arrogance/intransigence.

Politics has split families for 40 years--conservatives became the black sheep: alone, bewildered and in tears.

Liberals said there was nothing wrong with it. We could do it and God wouldn't have a fit: not legit.

Revive the incredible American dynamo: No taxes for working people, not letting globalists sell us out (evil).

They worship in vain, teaching as doctrines the commandments of men. math 15:9

Popularity does not determine truth--just the opposite.

Conformity to insanity, sadism and verbal abuse of the left: snap back or nature wipes you out instead.

The democratic party has never been so upset since the Republicans outlawed slavery. Alex Jones

TRUMP VS. GROUP

Americana: A system so good everyone adopted it willingly. Protestors are bought/divorced from reality.

Now we've won, our real work starts: Re-educate dumbed public, teach kids Civics and warm stony hearts.

Hollywood has lost all class. It's now a promoter of globalism and taking our guns but not theirs: the brass.

LEFT HATES OUR TRADITIONS AND CUSTOMS

The left wants to destroy our constitution, traditions/customs. They want us busted, or to be Muslims.

They parade like they're so superior: peas in a pod. Meanwhile they bash you a learned nerd as "odd".

The immoral Common Core stinks--turning sweet kids into sex pots--and it's disgusting beyond belief.

Liberals breaking down into conniption fits over devastating defeat when they thought they were elite.

Why do they love disorder and collapse? Because they're the devil, absolute evil: learn the facts.

Thanksgiving saw families fighting over politics: it happens when you're frantic and they're thick as bricks.

Our dinner guest was so self-discrediting but she may not see it for several years, God be willing.

What a moral vanity trip she was on! Virtue signaling while being a moron incapable of polite conversation.

She discredited herself so thoroughly and even got drunk over it. Wow, universities: you're filled with it!

Don't you understand, he has to play the game with cards held close, ok? Their ego blinds them to the fake.

TRUMP VS. GROUP

False doctrine is a filth, cancer and drought.

Obama's Whitehouse always sympathized with the killers, like thugs were his only emotional pillars.

You have to learn to stay apart from the mess: the church is full of ravenous wolves the bible confessed.

Everything in life—socially, emotionally, financially--tries to wear us down but with God, the crown.

THE DOUBLEMINDED ARE UNREWARDED

He won't receive a thing from the Lord bcuz he's double minded and unstable in all his ways.

Americans want competence not quotas.

The more they smear him the more I made the right decision cuz they're the problem/not solution.

The easily offended: easily manipulated and will always do crazy things to be accepted, never admitting it.

They don't feel we're in danger cuz they don't get the news--only state brainwashing, without a clue.

Why America's on the wane: Left wing policies brought staggering indebtedness impossible to maintain.

Now we really see who's dumb enough to go along with the herd. It lends discernment, a great barometer.

Soon we'll be rid of the filthy, debauched and sex-centered public schools and common core making whores.

I've been there, recall Vietnam? We were self-righteously angry too, but this new thing seems a scam.

Obama's "Medal of Freedom" was given out like lollipops to all his leftist friends/supporters though dumb.

TRUMP VS. GROUP

Clinton and Podesta see it as a war and in war people do get killed: no big thing blood and gore.

TV is only good for old movies. Modern movies reflect liberalism since the sixties: cheap, dirty and cheesy.

CRY BABIES/DUMMIES DON'T KNOW HISTORY

Cry babies and dummies don't know history: Immoral, debauched, tainted, brainwashed, immature, lazy.

The freedom that creates so many fantastic opportunities is hated by the left and the globalists.

They bought into the false paradigm 8 years ago, delusionally thinking they were winners by condoning sinners.

They are the racists: All the KKK (krazy kollege kids) see is skin color and it's very serious with these brawlers.

I think you're so shallow you liked him for his looks and style. He was "cool" so you didn't see the hostile/vile.

Nothing tastes so delicious as vindication, more than riches. It is them not us who were the evil witches.

We went through too darn much to just sweep it under the couch, calling us arrogant fascists and grouch.

They act so superior, saying "what you said was so disturbing" as if you're bad not those heartless cads.

Trump's transfer of power to the states will be transformational and that will appeal to the least rational.

The democrats want a permanent underclass.

They perverted our will and our kids. They made us accept the unacceptable so we self-medicated/lost our lids.

Liberals are indecent trash. If there's any doubt lets discuss each point and you'll see they're scum/out for cash.

TRUMP VS. GROUP

Trump will face the ridicule of treachery if he doesn't put Clinton misdeeds before a grand jury.

Don't be afraid, we're going to bring your country back. Donald Trump
HIX POLITIX UPDATES

Germany, compensating Nazi guilt, tells white citizens to prepare for demographic change/to be overrun.

Conservatives are just like everyone was in the 50's-60's before the hippies/feminist revolutionaries.

Tolerance and indulgence taken to absurd extremes is actually cruelty, brainwashing, being mean.

The people of Seattle are being asked to test out a theory that if police go away the crime goes away.

Outcomes: They want social justice not criminal justice and that's the beginning of the end like a holocaust.

Symptoms of addiction, mental illness or poverty are now **LEGAL DEFENSES** for crimes--"I was broke".

Assaults, harassment, trespass, breakins: crimes nullified cuz it's legal if you are a poor/crazy/addict.

People are convinced to do anything by shifting focus from the individual to the "good of the group".

That shift in focus from Christian/Americana individualism to the "good of the people" is entirely evil.

It's what **YOU** want not what's good for the others. Don't ever submerge yourself under the collective.

Would you talk out loud in a movie theater? Course not so please shut up when it's just me trying to hear.

HOMESTEAD UPDATES

TRUMP VS. GROUP

No one takes GLYCATION as their major diet matrix but I see it as central--delete signs of aging now.

Ha Ha: Coconut products are sky-high glycation, along with avocados, dairy, nuts, all oils, animal.

Look at food as INFORMATION which tells genes and DNA to turn off or on, hormones too, digestion.

Aristocratic Neatness is pure class and it's what I want in every room and drawer, the kitchen first.

How can we so desperately need meat, when billions live on rice and are much thinner/quicker please?

I don't want you to be gone in your sixties, I picture you being wheeled into ER from your meat feasts.

Millions die in their sleep but it's really from CHOKING and so I say: Just Skip Dinner and wake up lively.

My one addiction is Cheetos--so I may take a couple, so what. It's just the delicious taste I love.

Go ahead and eat your meat, it is none of my business anyway. I'd just hate to lose you suddenly.

Billions of people live on rice. They're thin and. quick, we're fat and sick so just think about this.

The racist globalists are trying to kill off all the minorities "so cursed" by giving them the vaccines first.

If you don't like your cherry smoothie add plant-based nonfat yogurt and lotsa dates in the blend.

100 KAREN KELLOCK BOOKS

AFFINITY OR MISERY
AGELESS CORNUCOPIA
AMERICA AWAKE!
AMERICA'S DAFT ERA
ARTS OF PALEO FASTING
AUTOPHAGY ON CHEATERS
BACKSTABBING NEUROTICS
BETRAYAL TRAUMA
BOOMERS AND BROKENNESS
BOOT ON NECK
CHAMPION GUIDES
COMMIE NUTHOUSE
COMMIES
COMMUNIST SPIRIT
CONTAGION OF MADNESS
CONTAGIOUS MADNESS
CULTURE CLASH BASHED
DAFT LEFT
DAILY FASTARIAN
DAM RATS
DIVERSITY IS CRUELTY
E-RACE WHITE
EVIL FREAKS (Beyond Gross)
THE END OR A BEND?
FEMALE BULLIES AND FEMI-NAZIS
FEMALE CARNALITY
FEMALE DUMB DOWN
FEMALE POWER DRIVE
FEMINISM AND RUIN 1 & 2
FIX FOR MISFITS
FOOLS & TRAMPS
FREEDOM SPEAKING
FRENEMY ENABLER
FRENEMY LIAR
FRENEMY THIEF
FRENEMY TRAITOR
TRENEMY TYRANT
GENIUS IS HELD DOWN
GLOBALISLAM
GOD USES THE FLAWED
HAZE OF THE LATTER DAYS

THE HERD IN WORDS
HIX POLITIX
HOW THEY RUINED US
JUST SKIP DINNER
LE FEMME AND THE COMMUNIST SPIRIT
LIBERAL CHAOS & ROT
LIBERAL DOUBLETHINK
LIBERAL GALL 1 & 2
LIBERAL SHOVE-DOWNS
LOCK YOUR GATE
LOSERS and Femme Fatales
MANUAL FOR SUPERIOR MEN
MODERN ART FROM HELL
MOSTLY FAKE
NOTES TO CHAMPS 1 & 2
OVERCOME FRENEMIES
PC MAKES US CRAZY
PEOPLE ARE CRUEL
PEOPLE PROBLEMS 1 & 2
PERSECUTED GENIUIS
POLI-PSYCH MYSTERIES
PRETENTIOUS SLOBS
QUEEN BEE
RED NEW DEAL
RETURNING TO FIRST NATURE
SEASON OF TREASON
SEPARATE MEANS HOLY
SOCIAL HYPNOTISM
SOLITUDE SOLUTION
SUPERCILIOUS
THE SCHOOLS SCREWED EM UP
TOAD TO PRINCE
TRIALS CYCLES
TRUMP VS. GROUP
TRUST IN TRASH
THE TRUTH ABOUT PEOPLE
UNDERHEANDEDLY CLEVER
WALK TALL WITHIN WALLS
WE'RE NOT ALL ONE
WINNERS SKIP DINNER
WORK OR SMERK

AUTHOR BIO
Karen Kellock Ph.D.

Ph.D Political Psychology, UCI 1976
Post-Doctoral: UCI Medical School
Department of Psychiatry
Grants NIMH, NIAAA

Ph.D. dissertation "A Systems-Theoretic View of Pathologic Interaction" made an early mark as the "Wife of the Alcoholic Syndrome". Postdoctoral research at UCI Medical, Dept. of Psychiatry on the systems surrounding pathology on NIMH and NIAAA federal grants: *The Contagion of Madness: The Psychology of Neurotic Interaction and Pathological Systems*. Therapy tool Therapeutic Playwriting introduced the play *Mary and Murv: Gruesome Twosomes in the Alcoholic Marriage*. She taught Abnormal Psychology and Pathological Systems Theory at UC and CSU campuses and developed "the Debris Theory of Disease" in five books and website: (www.karenkellock.org): *Champion Guides, Daily Fastarian, Just Skip Dinner, Arts of Paleo Fasting, Ageless Cornucopia. Manual for Superior Men is* a pick-it-up-anywhere book that you can't put down (20,000 Kellockialisms) and ever on your desktop it should be found (or this Ebook for superior wordsearch of new jargon).

www.ingramcontent.com/pod-product-compliance
Lightning Source LLC
Chambersburg PA
CBHW061731250726
48657CB00002B/875